The
FOOTPRINTS
of THE
SAVIOUR

J. M. Flanigan

Books by J. M. Flanigan

Hebrews (*What the Bible Teaches* Series)
Revelation

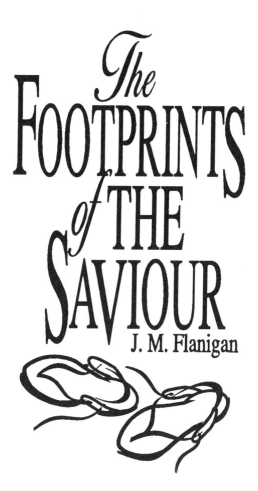

The
FOOTPRINTS
of
THE
SAVIOUR

J. M. Flanigan

GOSPEL FOLIO PRESS
P. O. Box 2041, Grand Rapids MI 49501-2041
Available in the UK from
JOHN RITCHIE LTD., Kilmarnock, Scotland

Originally printed as a series of articles in *Counsel Magazine*.

Cover design and photo by J. B. Nicholson, Jr.

Published by Gospel Folio Press
P. O. Box 2041, Grand Rapids MI 49501-2041

ISBN 1-882701-01-1

Printed in the United States of America

Not only on Judean hills,
Where He in distant ages trod,
Are seen the footprints of the Christ,
The wondrous Messenger of God;
For in the midst He walks today,
In busy lives, in quiet ways,
And speaks to every soul that hears
And fills each waiting heart with praise.
—T. Curtis Clark

Contents

Preface 9

1. Bethlehem 11

2. Nazareth 17

3. Cana 23

4. Sychar 29

5. The Mount of Olives 33

6. Bethany 39

7. Mount Hermon 45

8. Galilee 49

9. Jerusalem 55

10. The Emmaus Road 61

11. The Return to Galilee 65

Epilogue: He Ascended Up On High 69

Preface

It is our desire and intention, in the will of God, to trace that pathway which has brought so much pleasure to the Father. From Bethlehem where He was born, to Bethany where loving hearts made Him welcome; Sychar and Emmaus; Olivet and Hermon; Gethsemane; Golgotha; the Upper Room; the Garden Tomb; the Galilean Shore. It was "C.H.M." who said, "The study of the Lord Himself bows the heart in worship and fills the soul with wonder." May we behold His glory as we follow His footsteps from place to place.

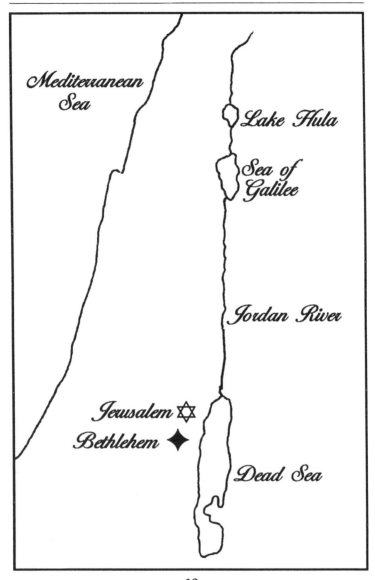

1
Bethlehem

The Birthplace of the King

The little town of Bethlehem lies about four or five miles south of Jerusalem on the way to Hebron. It is known locally as Beit Lahm, and is one of two Bethlehems in Israel. The other is Bethlehem HaGalilit, Bethlehem of Galilee, situated a few miles west of Nazareth, in the country of Zebulon. With inspired accuracy, the prophets and evangelists always speak of "Bethlehem of Judea," or "Bethlehem Ephratah" or "Bethlehem in the land of Judah," when referring to the birthplace of the Lord Jesus. They carefully distinguish the correct Bethlehem.

Bethlehem is first mentioned in our Bible in Genesis 35, in a tender story of a baby boy whose mother, Rachel, died when giving him birth. She named her baby "Benoni," which means "Son of my sorrow," but his father changed the name and called him "Benjamin," which means "Son of my right hand." So in its first mention there are anticipations in Bethlehem of a Babe who would be born to be a Man of Sorrows, but who would eventually sit down in glory at the Father's Right Hand. Our New Testament begins with Rachel's tears at the time of His birth (Matt. 2:18), but when all tears are ultimately wiped away, then Israel will rejoice in Him.

There are several references to Bethlehem in the book of Judges, particularly in a sad story of sin and shame so vile that we are happy to pass it by. But even this is a reminder that the sinless One who came to Bethlehem came indeed because of iniquity such as this.

How refreshing it is to turn to the book of Ruth, to find happier mentions of Bethlehem. Here is that delightful story of Naomi, of Boaz and Ruth, and eventually of a shepherd boy destined to be king. Did David play and work and sing and tend the flocks in the very fields where one day other shepherds with their sheep would stand in the presence of the glory and hear the angels announce the advent of Messiah? How little did the boy David realize that one day Bethlehem would be called the City of David, and the Babe of Bethlehem, the Son of David.

In the birth of the Saviour at Bethlehem we see the workings of divine sovereignty. Who would ever have imagined that Mary's Child would have been born there! Joseph and Mary lived some seventy miles away at Nazareth. It hardly seemed logical, or even sensible, that Mary, in such a condition, should (or could) undertake the journey to Bethlehem. Travel would be difficult, if not dangerous. Such a journey, at such a time, would be uncomfortable, undesirable, and most inconvenient. But sovereignty had purposed that the Son of Mary must be born at Bethlehem, and sovereignty accordingly arranged the circumstances.

There is a Caesar in Rome, and a carpenter in Nazareth, and God will use them both to fulfill His will. The Emperor is "Caesar the August," who thinks himself sovereign. In Rome, he is accorded divine honors. When he speaks, people must listen. When he issues decrees, his subjects must obey. He decrees that all his world must be enrolled. To facilitate this enrollment, men must register in the city of their fathers. The carpenter must register at Bethlehem. "The Most High ruleth in the kingdoms of men." The heart of the Caesar is in the hand of sovereignty. The decree that brings Joseph of Nazareth to Bethlehem is not Caesar's, but Jehovah's. And so the journey is made. They arrive at Bethlehem in obedience to the Emperor, and, says Luke, "so it was, that while they were there . . . she brought forth her firstborn Son." Divine purposes always come to pass. The Saviour is born—in Bethlehem of Judea.

There is not only *sovereignty* here, but *mystery* too. We bow in wonder. The Infant of the manger is the Ancient of Days, and we cannot understand it. The God of Eternity has come into time. The Lord of the Universe has come to Bethlehem. The God of Heaven is laid in a manger bed. All the fullness of the Godhead in a tiny infant body. He whose train filled the temple is wrapped in swaddling clothes. The Eternal One is born of a woman. The God of Sinai is born under the Law. He upholds all things, but is upheld by Mary. Worlds are dependent upon Him, but He is dependent upon a Hebrew maid and a Galilean carpenter.

Here is the apparent weakness of a Jewish Infant embracing all the Omnipotence of the God of creation. We do bow at the wonder of it. It is forever beyond our understanding. But when we cannot comprehend, we can still worship. Without controversy, great is the mystery . . . God manifested in flesh. We stand reverently at His manger cot, and adore Emmanuel come among us.

With *sovereignty* and *mystery*, there is also *poverty*. How poor they must have appeared for whom the crowded inn would not make room. How poor was that virgin mother who, herself, alone, wrapped her newborn in swaddling clothes, and herself laid Him down. No female companion at such a time as this. No human help! How poor! It was this poverty that later brought to the temple at Jerusalem, two doves or pigeons, as an offering. The same poverty made Him approachable, even to humble shepherds of Bethlehem who came to behold. In His poverty, He has come very near

13

to men. Though He was rich, yet for our sakes He became poor.

> *O ever homeless Stranger,*
> *Thus dearest Friend to me;*
> *An outcast in a manger,*
> *That Thou might'st with us be.*

But mingled with the *sovereignty* and the *mystery* and *poverty*, there is *glory*. One is born who has no link with Adam. He is virgin-born. He alone "came forth from the Father." Only the Son of Mary came voluntarily into the world. There is no fallen Adamic nature in Him. Children may be "partakers," by common lot, of flesh and blood, but He "took part" of the same, in a Manhood that was unique and apart. It is this that assures the glory of His impeccability and incorruptibility. He is the incomparable One, upon whom neither death nor disease nor deformity of any kind have any claim. Well might we say with the shepherds, "Let us now go, even unto Bethlehem, and see this thing which has come to pass."

> *Who is He in yonder stall,*
> *At whose feet the shepherds fall?*
> *'Tis the Lord, O wondrous story,*
> *'Tis the Lord, the King of Glory,*
> *At His feet we humbly fall—*
> *Crown Him, crown Him Lord of all!*

14

A shepherd leads his flock across the Judean Hills, near Bethlehem.

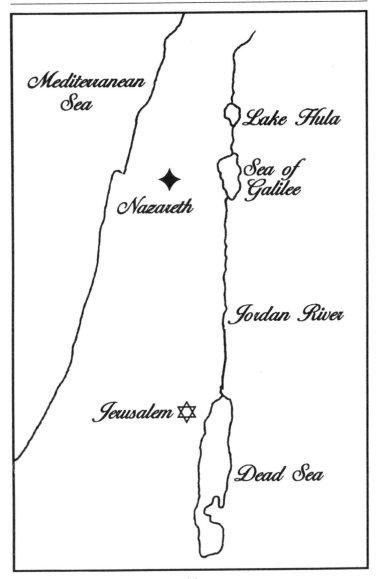

2
Nazareth

The Hidden Years

"Can there any good thing come out of Nazareth?"
"Come and see."   John 1:46

Well might Nathanael ask such a question, for he lived at Cana, only a few miles from Nazareth, and he knew Nazareth well. He knew its reputation, its sin, its physical and material and moral squalor. Nazareth! Never mentioned once in the Old Testament writings. Nazareth of the narrow streets; from whose higher ridges can be seen Nain and Endor, Tabor and Gilboa, and even Carmel and Hermon and Megiddo. Nazareth, stopping place of southward traveling merchants and traders who made it a nest of immorality and vice. Can there any good thing come out of Nazareth?

It is of wondrous, matchless grace that we may "come and see," that for thirty years there has lived here a Child, a Boy, a Youth, a Man, whose footprints have endeared Nazareth to the hearts of millions. Except for one brief but beautiful glimpse, there hangs a veil over these years, but enough has been afterwards recorded to help us to see and to adore.

Twenty times in our New Testament, the Saviour is called "Jesus of Nazareth." He is the Prophet of Nazareth too, and the Carpenter of Nazareth. Luke described the town as: "where He was brought up" (Lk. 4:16), and our Lord became known as "the Nazarene." It was an appellation of some stigma and contempt. The inhabitants of Galilee were not regarded favorably by their Judean neighbors, in whose eyes they were but peasants, unpolished, and even uncouth. The northern dialect drew the taunts of the people of the south, and there was a reproach for being a Galilean. But even in Galilee there was a general contempt for Nazareth, so that the question of Nathanael, the guileless Galilean, is understandable.

The holy footprints which we trace in Nazareth follow a pathway of mystery and beauty and glory, as inscrutable and incomprehensible as Bethlehem. How can the All-wise One increase in wisdom and stature? How can the sovereign, omnipotent One become subject to earthly guardians? How can the omnipresent One confine Himself for thirty years to a Galilean village? Where we cannot understand, we bow in worship—that He whose name is called "Wonderful" should be called "A Nazarene" for us.

> *I stand amazed in the presence*
> *Of Jesus the Nazarene,*
> *And wonder how He could love me,*
> *A sinner condemned, unclean.*

When, in the early days of His ministry, our Lord confronted the powers of darkness, the demon cried out, "Jesus of Nazareth . . . I know Thee, who Thou art, the Holy One of God" (Mk. 1:24). The demon saw what most men did not see; that behind the guise of the Carpenter there was Godhead glory in all its holiness and fullness. The Humble One was the Holy One. The Carpenter was the Creator. Jesus of Nazareth was Jehovah of Eternity. "I know Thee, who Thou art"!

In Nazareth, He began His spoken ministry. How often, during those thirty years, He must have quietly and reverently listened while others read His Prophets and expounded

18

His Law in that same synagogue. Then, on that memorable, historic sabbath, He stood up to read. Calmly He found the place and read the portion, handed the scroll to the attendant, and sat down to teach. "This day is this scripture fulfilled in your ears." Their Redeemer, Emancipator, and Healer of Broken Hearts, had come. He was their Prophet, Priest, and King. And He was—Jesus of Nazareth; their own Nazareth! But the door which had been closed against Him at Bethlehem was closed at Nazareth too. Again men said, "No room," and He was rejected. The synagogue at Nazareth, like the inn at Bethlehem, was closed to Him.

So our blessed Lord endured increasing reproach and contempt. Despised by Judeans for being a Galilean; despised by Galileans for being a Nazarene; and now despised by the men of Nazareth for His interpretation of divine truth. He left Nazareth, and came and dwelt in Capernaum, and though Capernaum became "His own city," yet still He was known as "Jesus of Nazareth." How often during the busy years that followed, the cry must have gone out, "Jesus of Nazareth passes by."

> And burdened ones, where'er He came,
> Brought out their sick and deaf and lame;
> The blind rejoiced to hear the cry—
> Jesus of Nazareth passeth by.

But the envy and venom of the leaders increased against Him, and eventually they came to the Garden to arrest Him. He took the initiative, and went forth to meet them. "Whom seek ye?" He asked. "Jesus of Nazareth," they replied. But Jesus of Nazareth is the "I Am" of Eternity, and they shrink backward and fall to the ground. They involuntarily recognize Him, the Deity which the demon had earlier seen, and they must bow in its awful Presence. But they took Him nevertheless.

In the hours that follow, His sorrows deepen. Bold Peter

19

quails before a maid who suggests, "Thou also wast with Jesus of Nazareth." The Lord looks and Peter weeps.

The night drags on and the morning comes, and with it His condemnation. They crucified Him. Pilate wrote a title, a superscription, an accusation. And the writing was: "This is Jesus of Nazareth . . ." In the languages of Jerusalem, Athens, and Rome, the Kingship of Jesus of Nazareth was proclaimed to all. But the real vindication must wait for three days.

On that glorious resurrection morning, the tomb is empty. An angel sits on the stone and declares, "Ye seek Jesus of Nazareth! He is risen; He is not here." And on that same day, as two disciples make their way to Emmaus, their conversation concerns "Jesus of Nazareth." Afterwards, in the early days of Gospel triumph, when Saul of Tarsus is blinded on the Damascus Road, and asks "Who art Thou, Lord?" the answer is simple—"I am Jesus of Nazareth" (Acts 22:8).

The links with Nazareth, then, persist even in the glory, which means that in His humility, in His deity, in His ministry, in His agony, and in His glory, the Saviour is content to be known as Jesus of Nazareth.

How grateful we are that He ever became a Nazarene.

He took my sins and my sorrows,
He made them His very own;
He bore the burden to Calvary,
And suffered, and died alone.

When with the ransomed in glory,
His face I at last shall see,
'Twill be my joy through the ages
To sing of His love for me.
                                        —C. H. Gabriel

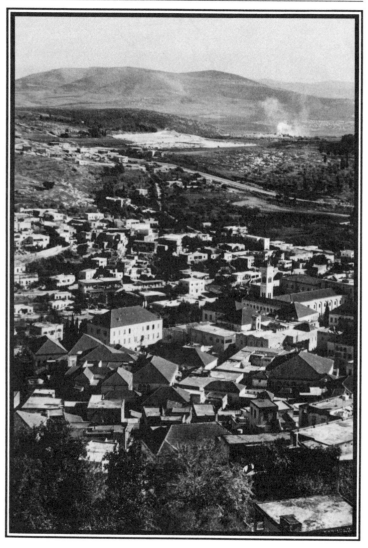

Nazareth perched atop the southern tip of the Lower Galilee Range.

21

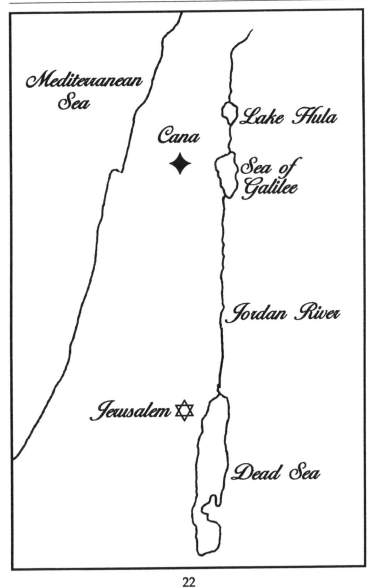

3
Cana

At the Wedding

Cana, a small upland town in lower Galilee, was the hometown of Nathanael. But, with the greatest respect to that guileless disciple, we remember Cana not because of him, but because it was here, not far from Nazareth, that our Lord began His miraculous ministry.

Only John records the story: a marriage; an invitation to Jesus and His disciples; a shortage of wine; and a manifestation of His glory that confirmed the faith of His followers. The glory that He manifested was many-splendored.

THE GLORY OF HIS GRACE

Only grace would have chosen Cana of Galilee for the inaugural Messianic miracle. Had the disciples been asked for their advice, had we been asked for ours, the answer would have been—"Jerusalem!" And not just Jerusalem, but the temple court. And not just at any time, but at a Festival time, when that court would be thronged with pilgrims. "That is the place, Lord," they would have said, "and that is the time." But He who delights to use small things, whose strength is made perfect in weakness, and who takes up weak things to

23

confound the mighty—He chose Cana—dusty, insignificant Cana of Galilee. Still, in our day, He delights to use the little things, and in His grace He makes them the instruments of His pleasure to display His glory. May we never become too big for Him to use.

THE GLORY OF HIS UNSELFISHNESS

Only a little while before this, He had been in the Judean wilderness. He had fasted for almost six weeks and was hungry. Yet, though there was apparently every good reason, He refused to turn stones to bread. The stones were His. He who would not turn stones to bread for His own necessity, turns water to wine for others' luxury. It was hardly a dire necessity that they should have more wine, but He saw their embarrassment and entered into their circumstances, and in that unselfish care for others which ever characterized Him, He wrought the miracle that met their need.

THE GLORY OF HIS SOVEREIGNTY

Sovereignty is supreme authority which cannot be questioned. Sovereignty cannot be commanded, nor directed. We cannot dictate to sovereignty; and here, in all the graciousness of the occasion, we see a display of our Lord's sovereignty.

His mother says, "They have no wine." It seemed such a simple comment, an observation. Yet anyone may read into it a suggestion that He should do something. All His life Mary had known who He was. For thirty years she had waited for His manifestation to Israel. Had she made similar suggestions to Him before, with insinuations and implications? "Woman —" He replies. It was not a disrespectful address to His mother; rather the opposite. He tenderly acknowledged her femininity, reminded her of it. This is not like Eden. The woman will not usurp the second Man, as Eve did the first. "Woman," He said, "what have I to do with thee?" He retains

His sovereign position and will act of His own volition when His moment comes. He does not receive orders from men.

THE GLORY OF HIS BOUNTY

"Fill the water pots with water"—and they filled them "up to the brim." How explicitly and immediately they obeyed, and how glad they must have been that they did. Because in the measure that they put in, He gave them back wine for water. From the cold stone water pots of old Jewish ceremonialism, He gave them the wine of joy, of a new Messianic age. They obeyed, and He rewarded accordingly. It is just the same today. As we put in, so we draw out. As we give our time, our talents, our possessions, our obedience, to Him, He gives back in abundance His own joy to us. To the extent that we respond and obey His Word, He brings gladness into our lives.

THE GLORY OF HIS DEITY

For thirty years there had lived in Nazareth a divine Person, but His essential, personal glory had been veiled in humanity. He had tabernacled in flesh. From this moment in Cana, there would be glimpses of that glory for those who were willing to see. Soon He will open blind eyes and deaf ears. He will unloose stammering tongues. He will deliver those held by demonism. He will even raise the dead in a display of divine majesty. Here, at Cana in Galilee, is the earliest manifestation of that glory.

Note that there was no collusion with His disciples. It was the servants who filled the water pots, not Peter and John. Note that it was the governor of the feast who commented on the excellency of the wine, not James or Andrew. There is independent, unsolicited testimony to the fact and the greatness of the miracle; and His disciples believed on Him.

Sixty years after the event, John wrote, "We beheld His glory." The dayspring from on high has indeed visited us.

25

Emmanuel has walked in Galilee. God has been among us. The Only-begotten has declared Him.

We bow in wonder and worship as we view His glory. May He become more precious, and our appreciation deepen, as we follow His footprints left in the land.

Cana, where the Saviour chose to begin manifesting His glory.

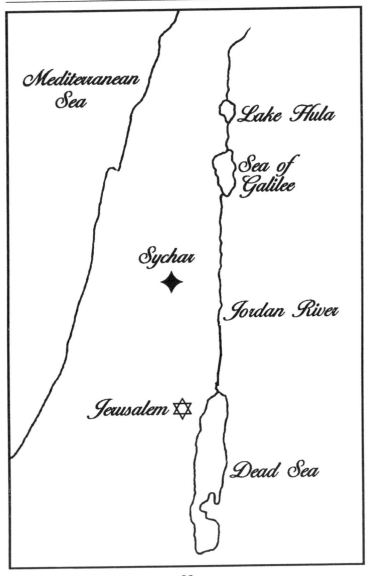

Mediterranean Sea

Lake Hula

Sea of Galilee

Sychar

Jordan River

Jerusalem ✡

Dead Sea

4
Sychar

Rendezvous at a Well

The same grace that brought our Lord to Bethlehem, and that took Him to Nazareth, and to Cana, now brings Him to Sychar in the Vale of Shechem. Having been rejected in Judea, He now comes as the Saviour of the world to Samaria. He "must needs" go that way. Now this was not at all a geographical necessity, that He should travel through Samaria. Although that was the most convenient and direct way from Judea to Galilee, it is well-known that the orthodox would not have used that route. Instead, they would have gone by Jericho and across the Jordan, up through Perea on the east bank of Jordan, and then back across the river into Galilee without touching the defiled Samaria at all. That He "must needs" go through Samaria was not a necessity of geography, but of grace. There was a poor Samaritan outcast there requiring help.

Our Lord arrived in the evening at 6:00 PM, for such is the sixth hour in the fourth Gospel. John, writing at the close of the first century, is using Roman reckoning of time, just as we do today. The sixth hour with John therefore, is either 6:00 AM or 6:00 PM and since 6:00 AM is not possible here, then it is an evening scene. It is not high noon, as suggested by some.

Being wearied, He sat thus on the well. Let us not miss that little word "thus." Arriving wearied, He sat thus—tired out, on the stone rim of the well. In three verses here our Lord is weary, thirsty, and hungry. The Son of God has become a true man, and in that lovely manhood which He has assumed He sits wearied on the well and requests a drink. What wondrous, indescribable grace is this, that the God of Israel should sit at a well in Samaria and ask a drink of a woman of Sychar.

How reminiscent is all this of the blessing of Joseph, given by Jacob in Genesis 49. "Joseph is a fruitful bough, even a fruitful bough by a well; whose branches run over the wall." Here at Sychar, near to a piece of ground that Jacob gave to his son Joseph, the ancient prophetic blessing was literally fulfilled. The heavenly Joseph is a fruitful bough indeed, His branches running over the wall of Judaism, carrying the sweet fruit of salvation to an outcast.

The woman is confused. She cannot understand how a Jew can make request of her, a woman, and a Samaritan. Nor, when He offers her "living" water, can she perceive that He is speaking of things spiritual. She thinks, no doubt, that the "living" water of which He speaks is the running water moving at the bottom of the deep spring well. How can He give her that water? She is occupied with water pots and buckets and material wells and running water until our Lord gently and graciously leads her on to greater things.

Her heart and desires having been aroused, He must now address her conscience. "Go, call your husband." Her brief answer is an acknowledgment of her guilt. "I have no husband." But no sooner is her conscience stirred than she tries to evade the issue. She will talk about worship, and places of worship, rather than pursue the matter of her sin, until the Lord brings her to the moment of truth. She needs salvation, but salvation is not to be had in places, or cities, or mountains, or temples. Neither in Jerusalem or Samaria; neither on

Mount Gerizim or Mount Moriah. Salvation is in a Person, and that Person was now speaking with her. The Man of Sychar was the Son of David and the Saviour of the world.

What steady progress does this poor woman make in her knowledge of Him during those moments at the well. When first she addressed Him, she knew him simply and only as "a Jew" (v. 9). He was, initially, just a man, a Jew, one of many. Did she know it by His dress? His appearance? His accent? At any rate, He was just, "a Jew."

After listening for a little while, she recognizes that this stranger is no ordinary Jew. She calls Him, "Sir" (v. 11). At the very least, He is a Jew worthy of respect and of courteous address. How many are there who accord to Jesus that same respect, but who never come to know Him as Saviour or Lord.

Still she listens, and so progresses in her apprehension. Now she says, "A Prophet!" (v. 19). What confession is this wrung from a Samaritan who recognized only Moses as a prophet. She had a small Bible, this woman of Samaria, which gave no place to Isaiah, or Daniel, or Zechariah, or Ezekiel, as prophets. Moses alone was their prophet. For her to say to Him, "A Prophet," was confession indeed. But still she must go further.

At the moment of His revelation of Himself she exclaims, "Messiah!" (v. 25); "The Christ!" (v. 29). She has found Him. Her heart is full. She can abandon water pots now, and in the newfound joy of salvation carry the news to others.

Oh, the grace of the Man of Sychar! Well did the late J. G. Bellett say, "He drinks of our pitcher to encourage us to drink at His Fountain."

31

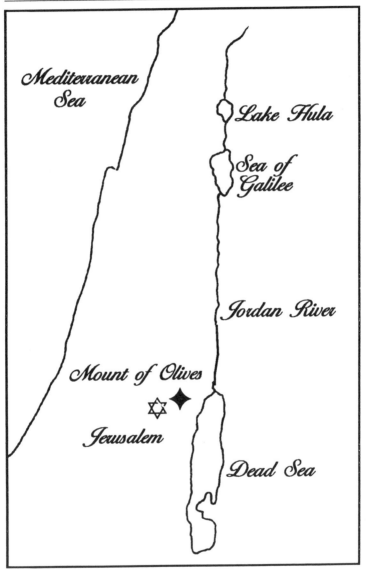

5
The Mount of Olives

Where He Resorted

It was Robert Murray McCheyne of Scotland who said, "If there is any place on earth where the physical scenery helps to an appreciation of divine things, it is the Mount of Olives." Olivet is saturated with tender memories of the Lord Jesus. It is wet with His tears and sanctified by His Footprints perhaps more than any other part of Israel.

The Mount of Olives is mentioned only twice in the Old Testament by name, though there are other allusions to it. In 2 Samuel 15, it is associated with a weeping nation and a rejected King David. In Zechariah 14, it is associated also with a weeping people as the King, the Son of David, returns to be vindicated. Other kings had made Olivet a "Mount of Offense," with their high places and idolatrous groves. When Jesus came, He made it a Mount of Prayer, of Priesthood, and of Prophecy; a Mount of Passion, of Power, and of Promise.

How often He prayed here. In the shelter and solitude of its olive gardens, how often He communed with Heaven. "As He was wont" (Lk. 22:39); "Jesus ofttimes resorted thither" (Jn. 18:2). Here, within sight of Jerusalem with all its noise and bustle, He found quiet. Here, with but a valley between Him and the Temple Mount, He found true sanctuary. And while, in the bustling city, the orthodox offered their repetitious prayers, He conversed, in silence, with the Father. He found solace here, from the empty, barren ritual of the nation's ceremonials; and while the city chanted on, He engaged in true intercession on the mount above it. He made Olivet a Mount of Prayer.

On the farther side of the Mount of Olives from Jerusalem was Bethany. What evenings of fellowship were enjoyed here! It was there they made Him a supper. It was there Mary sat at His feet. But it was there, at Bethany, on the eastern slope of Olivet, that they had seen His tears. Jesus wept on Olivet. They had sat at the feet of the Teacher here, and they had knelt at the feet of the compassionate Priest. Here at Bethany He had shared their sorrow. They had fellowshiped with Him in divine things and He had entered into their human sorrows. He had communicated Heaven's joy to them, and its comfort in their sadness. This was real priestly ministry. He had made Olivet a Mount of Priesthood.

Before leaving earth, our Lord gave two great final discourses. One of these was given to His own in the Upper Room. This little company was the nucleus of a new *Ecclesia* which He was to build, and in the Upper Room He spoke most privately and personally to them.

The other discourse was given on the Mount of Olives; we have come to call it, "The Olivet Discourse." Here He is speaking to the same little group, but our Lord is not now addressing them as the nucleus of the prospective Church. He speaks to them here as the Remnant of the Nation, and the discourse is full of instruction for a Remnant which will be, after the Church has been raptured Home. How beautiful that our Lord chose Olivet for the delivery of this great prophetic outline. Olivet, to which David had resorted when he too had been rejected, and a usurper had taken his throne. Olivet, to which Messiah will return one day in power and glory. This Olivet He chose as the platform from which to outline the future. He made Olivet a Mount of Prophecy.

But soon after that prophecy, the Mount was to see the beginnings of His Passion. Here, on Olivet, was Gethsemane.

> *Gethsemane, the Olive Press,*
> *And why so named let angels guess.*

In the agony of the Garden He assessed all the consequences of the sin of that first garden — Eden. Gethsemane is shrouded in mystery. It is the antechamber to Golgotha. It defies exposition, and we withdraw. Here, on Olivet's western brow, in the light of a Passover Moon, they come with lanterns and torches and weapons, to inaugurate a night of suffering that would reach to the noonday darkness of Calvary, and into the further mystery of the hours of sinbearing.

> *Garden of gloom appalling,*
> *Where in His sore amaze,*
> *Earthward in anguish falling*
> *Prostrate the Saviour prays;*
>
> *Prays in exceeding sorrow,*
> *Prays to the ground bowed low,*
> *Facing the dread tomorrow,*
> *Dark with unfathomed woe.*

The Mount of Olives had become His Mount of Passion.

Some weeks later, He led them to Olivet again. He was leaving earth; He was returning to the Father. As if reluctant to leave that place where loving hearts had made room for Him, "He led them out as far as to Bethany." From that spot Jerusalem was hidden. The ceremonies continued. The incantations and chants still resounded in the city. But on the other side of the hill, a great wonder is about to be enacted. He lifts His hands and blesses them. Then He begins to ascend. In defiance of natural law, and in defiance of demonic and Satanic energies, He passes through the heavens and into the heavens, in glory. He is Lord. He is supreme. And Olivet is the Mount of His Power.

As He ascends, His angels descend. They have a simple promise to leave at Olivet: "This same Jesus will come again." And so we wait. The Priest of Olivet, the Prophet of Olivet, will return to Olivet as King, and the Mount will be cleft in two at His coming. Before that, we expect Him to come for us, in accordance with His promise of the Upper Room, so that, when He returns to the Mount of Olives, we shall be with Him. In the day of His manifestation, we shall be manifested too. In the day of His triumph, we shall triumph. In the day of the gladness of His heart, we shall share His joy. He that shall come, will come, and will not tarry. That is the word which has made Olivet the Mount of Promise.

Well might we say, "How beautiful upon the mountains are the feet of Him that bringeth good tidings, that publisheth peace." Upon Zion; upon Moriah; upon the Mountains of Galilee and the Hills of Judea; but especially upon the Mount of Olives.

On the brow of Olivet, some 250 feet above Jerusalem's walls.

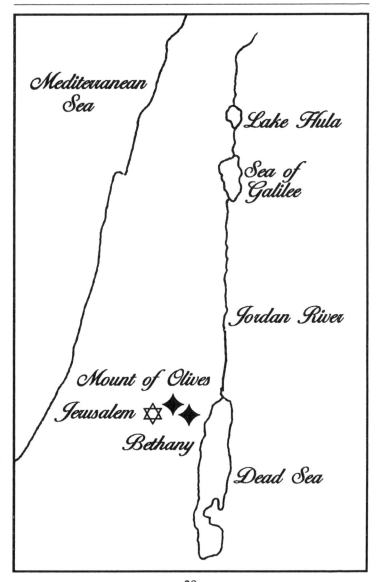

6
Bethany

A Home Away From Home

On the Eastern slope of the Mount of Olives, on the farther side from Jerusalem, and about two miles from that City, lies the village of Bethany. Today it is known as El Azariyah, the Town of Lazarus; sometimes it is called Betania. A dusty street or two; a few small dwellings; and a fragrance of Christ that lingers still. It was here that loving hearts made room for Him when others had rejected Him. It was here He found fellowship, and love, and appreciation of His Person.

There is a stony path from Bethany over Olivet and down into the city. How well our Lord knew this path. During His last week on earth, He walked it twice every day. In the morning, He came from Bethany over Olivet to Jerusalem. In the evening, He returned to lodge there. In a world that knew Him not, it was there at Bethany that He found a welcome.

Beginning with "Beth," the name Bethany means "The House of—," but the full meaning has become obscured. Indeed, there are no less than four suggestions. Some say, "The House of Sweetness." There are varieties of this, like "House of Dates," or "House of Figs." Others say, "The House of Sorrow," and yet others, "The House of Singing." Locally, however, it is agreed that the name means "The House of the

Poor," or "The House of Poverty." In fact, Bethany was all of these.

THE HOUSE OF THE POOR

Our Lord has begun His ministry with "Blessed are the poor in spirit." It is the opposite to pride. It is a man with poor thoughts of himself. How the Lord Jesus had taught His disciples that in the Kingdom things were different from what prevailed in the world. "He that is least among you shall be the greatest." But they had never learned. Still they disputed as to which of them should be the greatest. But at Bethany He was supreme. In the House of the Poor, He alone was great. The Bethany spirit exalts no one but Him. Men with the Bethany spirit have no rich thoughts of self; they are poor in spirit and have high thoughts of Christ only.

THE HOUSE OF SWEETNESS

At Bethany an ancient desire of Jehovah's heart was at last fully met. Centuries earlier, the God of the Hebrews had said, "Let My people go that they may *serve* Me." He wanted service. "Let My people go that they may *hold a feast* to Me." He wanted fellowship. "Let My people go that they may *sacrifice* unto Me." He wanted worship. But redeemed Israel often disappointed Jehovah, and still His heart yearned for a people who serve, fellowship, and worship. Until at last in a home in Bethany that same God of Israel sat incarnate, in the midst of adoring hearts who gave Him all His desire. Martha served; Lazarus sat; Mary worshipped.

Martha's service was appreciated by the Lord, who never complained about her (as preachers have done). It was just that, like many of us, the bustle of service had distracted her from Him. He showed her gently that there was something more than busy service.

Lazarus sat silent at the table. How he must have adored the Man who had raised him to new life. To sit quietly, meditatively, at the table with the Saviour was Lazarus' joy—the silence of communion with his Lord. Lazarus never speaks, at least, not in the records; not one word. Of him it is simply said that he sat at the table with Him. This is fellowship indeed.

Mary teaches us how to worship. She breaks her alabaster flask of precious sweetness on the Saviour's person. With a fragrance which John calls "very costly," she pours her love upon Him, and fills the house with it too. She must have had it clinging to her own self as well. It is the sacrifice of praise. It is the extravagance of love which does not stay to calculate, but lavishes its store upon the loved ones. In the house of sweetness, our Lord found service, and fellowship, and worship.

THE HOUSE OF SORROW

Those who love Him are not immune to suffering. The choicest saints have known their share of sorrow, and it was so at Bethany. There was sickness, anxiety, bereavement, and sorrow. In His wisdom, and in the working out of His plan for them, Jesus tarries at Bethabara while they wait for Him at Bethany. They cannot understand His delay. As yet they do not know that it is because He loves them, and that all things work together for good to them that love Him. Lazarus dies. Our Lord's word to Martha is simple. "If you will believe, you will see the glory." Trust, and wait, and watch, and eventually see the glory of His purpose for you. And so it was, that out of the sorrow came the Bethany which bore the sweetness that we have seen.

THE HOUSE OF SINGING

It is not to be wondered at, that when the Lord Jesus was leaving the earth in the Ascension, He chose to leave from Bethany. It was as if He would linger longest at the spot where He had been made welcome. And from the slopes of

Olivet, at Bethany, He went up in glory. He left them with the joy He had promised them, and in that joy they returned from Bethany to Jerusalem. It was a house of singing. The Lord had gone up, and gone in, and He had blessed them as He went up. There was a Man in the Glory, gone up from Bethany, and their hearts were full.

May our hearts, our lives, our homes, our assemblies, be like Bethany. May we give that blessed Man place for whom earth still has no room.

Near Bethany, a cloud received the Lord out of the disciples' sight.

43

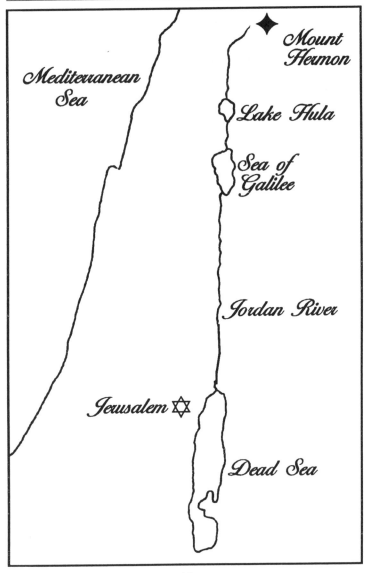

7
Mount Hermon

The Great Question

The mountains of Israel are steeped in history, shrouded in mystery, and hallowed with a certain glory. In some senses, Hermon dominates them all. The highest mount in the region, it towers to nearly 10,000 feet on Israel's northern border. It is eternally capped with snow. It is a most fitting reminder of the majesty of the scenes which were enacted on its southern slope. Here, where the Jordan has its source, is Caesarea Philippi. Here Peter made his great confession of Matthew 16, and here, it would seem, was the transfiguration scene of Matthew 17.

Our Lord chose Hermon and Caesarea Philippi as the place in which to ask the immortal question, "Whom do men say that I the Son of Man am?" Why did He choose this particular spot for such a question?

Caesarea Philippi was originally known as Panias, named after the pagan god Pan. This was Galilee of the Gentiles. There was a sanctuary here, in which was an idol-image of Pan. Philip the Tetrarch, son of Herod the Great, rebuilt the city of Pan, and named it after his Caesar, Tiberias. There was another Caesarea, however, on the coast, so to distinguish them, what more selfish, gratifying way than to associate his own name with Caesar's, and call the rebuilt city "Caesarea Philippi." On the rock of Hermon, above the city, Philip erected a majestic white marble temple in honor of Caesar, and, as well as this, there were perhaps fourteen other temples in the area, built in honor of various Syrian gods.

In the midst of all this confusion of pagan deities, our Lord asked His question, "Whom do men say that I . . . am?" Public opinion was varied. There were some who wondered if the martyred John Baptist had reappeared. There were those who saw in Jesus some likeness to Elijah: "Some say that Thou art Elias." Had others witnessed His tears and heard His tender pleadings? It reminded them of the weeping prophet and they suggested, "Jeremias." Others simply thought that He was a prophet.

But our Lord now makes the question personal and piercing. "But ye, whom say ye that I am?" Peter answered boldly, "Thou art the Christ, the Son of the Living God." There was no doubt and no hesitation. Messiah had come. This was He. Amid the relics of dead deities, the Son of the Living God stood in power. In the shadows of the heathendom which had corrupted the great Mount, Jesus is confessed supreme. Upon this rock He would build His Church, and Hermon would be remembered as the place of the great confession.

After six days, Jesus ascends the Mount. Peter, in retrospect, calls it, "The Holy Mount" (2 Peter 1:18). With Peter, James, and John, our Lord will climb these slopes. They will be permitted to see His glory.

There were at least three reasons for this display of majesty which we have come to call "the Transfiguration."

Firstly, there was what might be termed a *moral* reason. It was for the personal, human comfort of the Lord Jesus. About to be cruelly, callously, and unjustly condemned by the nation, He would be comforted by the approbation of Heaven. The Father would express His delight in Him. The heavenly visitors would intimate that the conversation of Heaven was

46

about His forthcoming exodus which He would accomplish. Heaven was in accord with the Father and the Son, no matter what men or Israel would think or do.

Secondly, there was a *dispensational* reason for the Transfiguration. This little Jewish remnant that accompanied Him saw "His majesty" (2 Peter 1). They saw the Kingdom. If it was not yet the time for reigning, for tabernacles, or for permanent glory, well, at least that was coming. They had a preview. And if they were soon to see the King hanging upon a cross, thorn-crowned and bleeding and disrobed, still, they had the sure promise. The eventual glory was assured. They had seen it. The King would be, must be, vindicated one day, when what they saw on the Mount was fulfilled.

Then there was a *practical* reason for it. These three disciples were destined for great things, and for suffering too. Peter would soon become the Pentecostal preacher, announcing the glory of Jesus crucified, risen, and ascended. James would be an early martyr, within the next twelve or fourteen years. John would linger on into old age to become the sole survivor of the apostolic band. He was to be, too, the great apocalyptic writer, the seer. They all needed encouragement. This was it, a sight of His glory which they would never forget.

It was proper that Moses should be there. He too, had once climbed a mount with three men, and his face had shone. His types were now about to be fulfilled in Jesus, and his rites and ceremonies were to be done away. It was fitting that he should appear to see the radiant face of the blessed Man to whom all his writings had pointed.

Elijah also was there, type of the great Forerunner of the Messiah. Elijah and Moses, representing all the law and the prophets, are about to be eclipsed by the glory of the Son.

The face of Jesus shone. This was inherent, personal glory that radiated from Him. It was not reflected glory such as lighted the face of Moses. And what is glory? How difficult it is to define. But someone has called it, "The outshining of an inner excellence." That is what they saw, and with the glory cloud and the voice from out of it, they were sore afraid. Gently He touched them and said, "Be not afraid." How tenderly can the Lord of Glory comfort His people.

And on the slopes of the Holy Mount they saw no man save Jesus only. May the atmosphere of Hermon fill our hearts and our assemblies, and help us to give to Him the unique and solitary place. May the dew of Hermon bring spiritual prosperity and refreshment to our ofttimes barren hearts.

8
Galilee

Liquid History

How pleasant to me thy deep blue wave,
O Sea of Galilee!
For the glorious One who came to save
Hath often stood by thee.

Graceful around thee the mountains meet,
Thou calm reposing sea;
But ah! far more, the beautiful feet
Of Jesus walked o'er thee.

The hills and valleys and the Sea of Galilee are radiant with memories of the Lord Jesus. Around this lovely lake, and especially on its northwest shore, were so many of the scenes of our Lord's ministry: Capernaum, Bethsaida, Chorazin, Magdala, Tabgha, Gadara, The Mount of Beatitudes, the storm, the miraculous catch of fishes, the walking on the waters. As Dr. Thompson says, "The blessed feet of Immanuel have hallowed every acre, and the eye of divine love has gazed a thousand times upon this fair expanse of lake and land."

The sea is harp-shaped, or pear-shaped, measuring about thirteen miles by eight miles, widest and deepest at its northern end. Physically, it is surpassingly beautiful; a golden beauty in the morning and evening hours, and in the daytime an exquisite jewel of blue lying on the bosom of Immanuel's Land. It is variously known as "the Sea of Galilee," "the Sea of Tiberias," "Gennesaret," and "Chinnereth" or "Kinnereth." This last is the Hebrew word for "harp." The lake nestles among green and brown hills. Today there is tranquility and quietness, but in our Lord's day there was bustling activity in the once populous cities which were around the shore.

TIBERIAS

The only town today on the lakeshore, Tiberias, was built by Herod Antipas and named after his Caesar. It is interesting that there is no record of our Lord having visited Tiberias, or of having ministered there. It was a predominantly Roman town. He was sent to the lost sheep of the House of Israel. Besides, Tiberias was built over the site of an old cemetery; no true Jew would have desired to live there.

CAPERNAUM

Here our Lord made His home when He was rejected by the men of Nazareth (Matt. 4:13). At that time, "walking by the Sea of Galilee," He called Simon and Andrew to be fishers of men. But it is a sad reflection on the moral conditions at Capernaum that although they were to reject the Saviour, yet there was "in their synagogue" a man with an unclean spirit. Our Lord graciously delivered him. It was here too, at Capernaum, that He healed Peter's mother-in-law of a fever, and then, in the evening, when the sun was setting, delivered many from disease and demon-possession. Here lived the man whom we have come to know as "the sick of the palsy," and this Capernaum was also the home of the nobleman whose sick son was healed by a word spoken some twenty miles away at Cana (Jn. 4). And did the centurion know of this, who, when the Lord was in Capernaum, sent that word of faith to Him, saying, "Lord, trouble not Thyself . . . but say in a word, and my servant shall be healed?" What mighty works were done here in Capernaum. But they rejected Him, and He pronounced their doom (Matt. 11). Today there is nothing but ruin, a sombre monument to their unbelief.

> *Tell me, ye moldering fragments, tell,*
> *Was the Saviour's city here?*
> *Lifted to heaven, has it sunk to hell,*
> *With none to shed a tear?*

MAGDALA

Galilee appears to have been plagued with demonism and the blight of unclean spirits. At Magdala lived Mary, whom now we know as "the Magdalene." Somewhere here by the lakeside she met the Lord. He delivered her from demon possession. Seven demons! She was completely in their power. But He emancipated her, and it seems that from that moment she never left Him. In her undying devotion, she stood weeping by His tomb in the garden, saying, "My Lord . . . tell me where thou hast laid Him." Magdala today is a tiny village amid the trees, but the sweetness of the memories abide.

GADARA

On the other side of the lake lived "Legion," the demoniac who dwelt among the tombs. He too was delivered by the shore. His tormentors rushed the swine into the blue waters, and left him sitting at the feet of Jesus, clothed, and in his right mind.

THE MOUNT OF BEATITUDES

Somewhere on the northern shore of the Sea of Galilee our Lord gave the "Sermon on the Mount," and somewhere He also gave us the Kingdom Parables of Matthew 13. The Sermon on the Mount begins with what we call "the Beatitudes," so the traditional site of that ministry has become known as

"The Mount of Beatitudes." Our Lord's ministry began with the pronouncement and promise of blessing. The Old Covenant writings had concluded with the word "curse" (Mal. 4:6). Those were the writings of Moses the Law-Giver, and his fellow prophets. But grace and truth came by Jesus Christ and by the tranquil Sea of Galilee He said, "Blessed are ye . . . Blessed are ye . . . Blessed are ye . . ." (Matt. 5) The "Stranger of Galilee" had come with blessing; not to condemn. However, His gracious words and ministry were largely rejected, and He had to outline, in parable form, the course and character of the Kingdom during the days of His forthcoming rejection and exile. He chose the Galilean shore for that discourse too.

THE STORM

Every afternoon there is a storm of sorts on Galilee. The temperatures drop; the winds come through the valleys and stir the waters. At times it is trivial; at times it is severe. It was on one such occasion that He slept in the storm. Asleep on a pillow! More correctly, it was "the" pillow. The only pillow? The Captain's pillow? He was Master of the Storm, and of the ship, and of their fears, and He calmed the tempest. Still He is Lord of the storm. Still, to many a troubled heart He would say, "Peace, be still." And the troubled sea that would frighten us He would still put beneath His feet.

The memories linger on, of the lovely Man who walked by the Sea of Galilee; who healed the lepers there; who fed the multitudes; who comforted the widow; and who, in it all, brought so much pleasure and joy to His Father's heart.

> *O Galilee, sweet Galilee,*
> *I love your hills and vales and sea;*
> *I love the Christ you gave to me;*
> *O Galilee, sweet Galilee.*

Sunrise over the Sea of Galilee, still plied by little fishing boats.

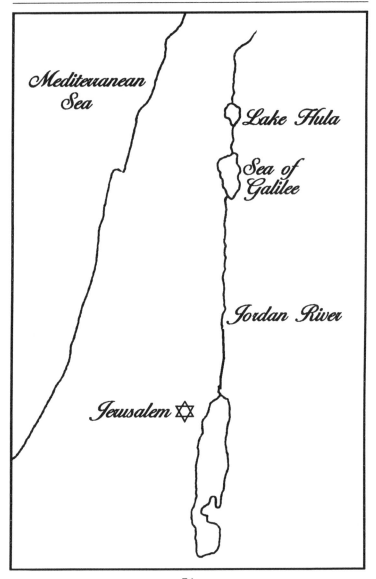

9
Jerusalem

City of the Great King

Our Lord ever walked with Jerusalem in view. Wherever He might be in gracious ministry, He would ultimately return to Jerusalem to die outside its walls. It would become, eventually, the city of His Tears, His Trial, His Tree, and His Tomb. He set His face to go to Jerusalem. Matthew puts the story of those last hours at Jerusalem between the "evenings" (Matt. 26:20; 27:57). John puts the story between the "gardens" (Jn. 18:1; 19:41).

Some years ago, on a visit to Jerusalem, I was asked to speak to a little company of believers on the subject of the sufferings of Christ. The meeting was to take place in the Garden, near the Tomb. I prayed for some fresh approach to the precious, familiar story of our Lord's sorrows as I perused the Gospels. It came to me that there must have been at least fifteen hours of suffering between the Garden of Gethsemane and the Garden Tomb where they buried Him. I read again and again the records of Matthew, Mark, Luke, and John, comparing and contrasting. After some time, some words from these chapters seemed to group themselves in my mind. I jotted them down. Later, when I counted them, I found that I had fifteen words. Fifteen words seemed to tell the story of fifteen hours of suffering on that last night. The words were these:

The Silver, The Sweat, The Spitting, The Smiting, The Stripping, The Scourging, The Sentence, The Shame, The Spike, The Superscription, The Sin-bearing, The Sponge, The Spear, The Sepulcher, and The Stone.

THE SILVER

The counting out of thirty pieces of silver to Judas began the night of suffering. In Israel's laws for compensations (Ex. 21:32) it was the price of a slave. Men bartered and bargained, and finally agreed the Saviour's value at thirty pieces of silver. Man's estimate of the worthy One was very low. He who was inestimably precious to God was valued by men at just the price of a slave.

THE SWEATING

Gethsemane means "The Oil Press." Here the olives were crushed, and here, in the mysterious conflict of those last hours, our Lord sweat "as it were" great drops of blood. It was not that He perspired blood, or even blood-tinged sweat, but rather that His perspiration, in His agony, fell from His brow as heavy as blood drops. He prayed "more earnestly," a stone's cast from His disciples; like the Holy Ark of earlier days, He was distanced from the people. His holy sweat moistened the ground of Gethsemane's Garden, as did His tears until, in the late evening, they arrested Him, betrayed with a kiss.

THE SPITTING

Across the Kidron was the House of Caiaphas the High Priest. They took Jesus bound there, and there they spat on His face. The spittle has ever been the most foul form of insult among men. With certain animals it is their way of expressing hostility and enmity. In their baseness they spat on our Lord.

How tenderly amazing it is, that the Father should have watched in silence while men did that to His Beloved.

THE SMITING

How literally they fulfilled so many scriptures. They smote the Judge of Israel upon the cheek (Micah 5:1). They buffeted Him. The gentle One who will not retaliate is pushed and jostled and struck by puny, but wicked, men. From the House of Caiaphas, in the early morning hours, our Lord was taken to Gabbatha. Here was the Fortress of Antonia, built on the corner of the Temple mount. Here was Pilate's Judgment Hall, and here the sorrows continued.

THE STRIPPING

They took His own clothes from Him, and dressed Him in purple. They did not know, of course, that in earlier times, when Israel was on the move in the wilderness, the Golden Altar was covered with a purple cloth (Num. 4:13)! He, from whom there had ever ascended a sweet fragrance to God, was now stripped of His Galilean garments and draped in purple.

THE SCOURGING

At the whipping post they scourged Him. "The plowers plowed upon My back: they made long their furrows" (Ps. 129:3). "I gave My back to the smiters" (Isa. 50:6). Not Jewish scourging this, which would have been limited to forty stripes (Deut. 25:3). This was Roman Scourging, limited only by the whim of the soldiers, and by the time at their disposal.

THE SENTENCE

He, who only was entitled to live, was condemned to die. "Crucify Him!" And Pilate gave sentence. The Prince of Life is sentenced to death. Man, who in Eden had forfeited his right to live, condemns Him to die who had no link with either Eden or Adam. "Take ye Him, and crucify Him!"

THE SHAME

Crowned with thorns, carrying His cross, our Lord leaves Jerusalem. Amid the taunts and ribald laughter, He hides not His face from the shame of it. The theme of angels' praise becomes the song of the drunkard. But He despised the shame—despised the despising, thought nothing of the fact that they thought nothing of Him—"for the joy that was set before Him" (Heb. 12:2).

Beneath an Eastern sky;
Amid a rabble cry;
A Man went forth to die;
For me!

Thorn-crowned His lovely Head;
Blood-stained His every tread;
Cross-laden, on He sped;
For me!

THE SPIKE

"They pierced My hands and My feet." Crude, coarse, spikes of iron, were the nails with which they nailed Him there, at the place of the skull, and having crucified Him, they put over His Head:

THE SUPERSCRIPTION

"This is Jesus of Nazareth, the King of the Jews." It was a superscription, called by Matthew, "His Accusation," but by John, "His Title," for so it rightly was.

THE SIN-BEARING

At bright noonday the sun withdraws its light. In the darkness that covers the earth the Saviour suffers what we cannot know. "He bare our sins in His own body on the tree." Man is closed out. God and the Holy Sin-bearer are alone in the darkness, and from the shadows the orphan cry — "My God, My God . . ." Where we cannot understand, we bow in wonder and worship.

THE SPONGE

He cries, "I thirst." When His ministry began, He had sat on a well asking, "Give Me to drink." Now, at the close of that ministry, He hangs alone upon His cross saying, "I thirst." A sponge is filled with vinegar, the sour wine, the common drink of the Roman soldier. It is put to His lips in literal fulfillment of Psalm 69:21, and He cries, "It is finished."

THE SPEAR

They pierced His side with a lance. As the late Harold St. John has said, "A highway has been opened to the heart of God." And for the skeptic and scoffer and cynic of a later day it can be said, that man has, with that spear, provided his own proof that Jesus really died. One day they shall look on Him whom they pierced.

THE SEPULCHER

Near to the Skull Hill was the rock-hewn tomb, nigh to the city, but outside. In the late afternoon they laid Him there.

> *Spices most sweet they chose;*
> *Aloes they brought, and myrrh;*
> *Wound Him with these in linen clothes,*
> *Gave Him a sepulcher.*

THE STONE

It sealed His tomb, for just a little while. Soon it was rolled away and an angel sat upon it, declaring, "He is not here." The Man of Sorrows was risen and alive! His tomb was empty.

In the City of the Great King our Lord had suffered, and outside its gate He had died. It was the only night, in the records of His life, that He had spent inside the walls of Jerusalem. Now the desolate city awaits His return. One day, in power and glory, He will come back. "Lift up your heads, O ye gates." The King of Glory will one day get His rightful place, and Jerusalem shall be the City of Peace once more.

The southwest corner of the Temple Mount area in old Jerusalem.

10
The Emmaus Road

Walking With Jesus

Emmaus! A small village some seven miles from Jerusalem, today it is known as Amwas. The place is as insignificant as were Bethany and Cana, but the Saviour was there, and this has made the difference and has preserved Emmaus in our memories and in our affections.

It would be easy to believe that the two disciples were husband and wife. They walked the path of life together; they communed together and reasoned. Recent events had saddened their circumstances and their conversation, and it showed in their countenances (Lk. 24:17). Their Jewish dreams had, in one day, been shattered. Their bright hopes had been dimmed. They were disillusioned, dispirited, and forlorn. It was likely with a slow and heavy pace that they trudged the dusty road from the Holy City to Emmaus. They had walked it often before, but never in such despondency as now. They were doubters. "We trusted," they said. Their trust was in the past tense. After three lonely days they had abandoned hope. It was as if the darkness of Golgotha still prevailed.

But as they walked in their sorrow, "Jesus Himself drew near and went with them." Oh, the beauty and accuracy of

Holy Scripture! Not just "Jesus drew near," but "Jesus *Himself.*" He who had but recently told them, "The Father *Himself* loveth you" (Jn. 16:27); He, of whom it is said, "The Lord *Himself* shall descend from heaven with a shout" (1 Thess. 4:16); He, of whom it is written, "Jesus *Himself* stood in the midst of them" (Luke 24:36); it was this *Jesus Himself* and not another who drew near, and went with them. How personal is His affection for His sorrowing people! He joins them on the Emmaus Road.

Graciously the Lord will allow them to unburden their hearts to Him. He helps them to do so—asking questions, inviting answers. They marvel that He must be the only sojourner in Jerusalem who was apparently not aware of the things that had happened there in recent days. How often we underestimate the Lord. He who had been the central figure in the whole sad story now hears them ask, "Art Thou only a stranger in Jerusalem, and hast not known?"

Still, in tender love and patience, He draws them out. "What things?" He asks. And they rehearse it all to One who knows it so well. "Jesus of Nazareth, mighty in deed and word." Betrayed! Condemned! Crucified! Dead! The Redeemer of Israel dead! And buried! Now, today, the third day, reports of an empty tomb, but "They found not His body" (v. 23). "Him they saw not" (v. 24). They are finished now. The story is told.

How gentle the Lord is, even in reproving. If only they would believe "all" that the prophets had spoken, not just that glory part which they wanted to believe. The entrance to the desired glory is inevitably arrived at by an avenue of suffering. "Ought not Christ to have suffered these things?" And so begins that sweetest of all Bible readings, as from Moses and the Prophets, the Psalmists and the Poets, He shows them that all the Scriptures relate to Him, and they have lived to see the glorious fulfillment of so many of the sacred predictions. Abel's sacrifice, Isaac's altar, the Paschal lamb, the brazen serpent, the Levitical offerings, Psalms 22 and 69, Isaiah 53, Zechariah 12, Daniel 9. These, and a multitude of other scriptures, had pointed to these days, and had been fulfilled before their very eyes. "O . . . slow of heart to believe."

Engrossed in His holy exposition, they had covered the miles and had arrived at Emmaus. The sun was setting over the distant hills of Moab. In perfect courtesy, the Stranger made as though He would have gone farther, but they constrained Him with the immortal "Abide with us." For us, as for them, the day is far spent. Politically, prophetically, and for some of us, personally, the sun is going down. How much we need His presence. He responded to their plea and went into the Emmaus home to tarry with them.

The Divine Guest soon becomes the Host. In a quiet and gracious manner, He presides at their table and breaks the bread. Then! Did they recognize the familiar thanksgiving? Or did the full sleeves of His garment fall back as He handled the loaf, to reveal the nail prints? He was made known to them in the breaking of bread. Oh, that it might be more often true of us as we sit at the Supper!

> *Thou glorious Bridegroom of our hearts,*
> *Thy present smile a heaven imparts;*
> *Oh, lift the veil, if veil there be,*
> *Let every saint Thy beauty see!*

It is the chapter of the opened eyes (v. 31), the opened Scriptures (v. 32), and the opened understanding (v. 45). And having revealed Himself, He vanished out of their sight.

"Did not our heart burn within us . . . ?" they recalled. Note the singular "heart," not "hearts." Were they, then, husband and wife indeed?

With what joy they hasted to Jerusalem, bearers of the message which had, in fact, already reached the eleven. "The Lord is risen indeed." Still it is our privilege to carry to the world, and to His people, the message of a risen Christ. And still it is our privilege to have Christ, the risen Christ, "abide with us." He is the Christ of Emmaus still, though exalted in the heavens.

Like the two on the road, many still do not recognize their Messiah.

11
The Return to Galilee

Keeping the Appointment

Our Lord was a Galilean. So were eleven of His disciples. He had lived in Galilee for the greater part of thirty years. His miraculous ministry had begun in Cana of Galilee. His "Sermon on the Mount" had been delivered in Galilee, as were His Parables of the Kingdom (Matt. 13), and so much more of His spoken ministry. He had walked on the Sea of Galilee, and He had walked and talked on the lakeshore. The maid in the palace court had called Him "Jesus of Galilee" (Matt. 26:69). It is hardly surprising then, that, risen from the dead, our Lord would want to meet His loved ones in Galilee.

On His last evening with them, He had promised His disciples: "After I am risen again, I will go before you into Galilee" (Matt. 26:32). The angel at the empty tomb had confirmed this, "He goeth before you into Galilee" (Matt. 28:7). The Lord Himself had repeated it to the women, "Galilee . . . there shall they see Me" (Matt. 28:10). And accordingly the eleven met Him on the appointed mountain slope in Galilee (Matt. 28:16).

But perhaps one of the loveliest of Galilean pictures is that of John 21. The chapter has been called "The Epilogue" to John's Gospel. It was not written to prove that Jesus was alive; that had been proven in John 20. John 21 has been given to us to demonstrate that the Risen Christ desires to enter into the affairs of our daily lives. Though now ascended, He is not remote and far removed from His people: "Lo, I am with you alway." How many of us believe unreservedly that He is risen, but do not practically appreciate His living presence in our lives?

Seven disciples were "together." What a lovely word. "How good and how pleasant it is for brethren to dwell together in unity" (Ps. 133:1). In spite of vastly different personalities and temperaments, they were "together." Peter is first mentioned. This impetuous, impulsive, lovable man is a leader of men. But the old "Simon" is attached to his name. There is much of the old nature yet.

Thomas is with them; Thomas, melancholy, pessimistic, doubting, ever looking on the blacker, sadder side of things (Jn. 11:16; 14:5; 20:25).

Nathanael, too, was there: the guileless, openhearted Israelite with no Jacob in him (Jn. 1:47). And John the beloved was there, with James, his brother, soon to become a martyr, faithful unto death (Acts 12:2).

Two others were with them; anonymous men, and the suggestion has been made that where we find such anonymity there is opportunity to put ourselves into the picture. What variety then, of men who loved the Master, and, in His absence, they were "together."

Peter gives the lead. How responsible are leaders! "I go a fishing," he said. "We also go with thee," said the others. Were they all too quick? Should they not have waited for the Lord? We would not be critical, but what we do know is this, that they went forth with neither His precept, His promise, nor His presence, and that night they caught nothing. One wonders about the conversation of that long night. Did they talk about Him? Were there many reminiscences? Did they share the memories and experiences of those eventful three years that were past? In any case, they caught nothing.

But eventually the morning came, and Jesus stood on the shore. They failed to recognize Him. In the bustle of service, it can be true of us, too, that we lose sight of Him. Martha was "distracted" with much service. May we never be so busy that we are distracted from Him whom we serve.

He obtains from these weary men a painful acknowledgment of their failure. "Have ye any meat?" They answered Him, "No." But our acknowledgment of our failure is simply His opportunity to enter into our lives. His strength is made perfect in weakness. They obey Him implicitly, and their reward is immediate; a net full of fishes; and all of them great! And an unbroken net too! Some of them would recall a similar incident in our Lord's early ministry (Lk. 5). "It is the Lord," says John. Note that it is love that first recognizes Him.

With His own hands He has prepared a fire, with fish and bread. "Come and dine," He invites them. There are other things to be attended to, and to be talked over, but first, in gracious and kind consideration, He will feed them, and warm them. It would seem that a silence ensues while they eat.

Jesus breaks the silence. "Simon, son of Jonas, lovest thou Me more than these?" Do you really love Me more than these men do? You once boasted that you did (Mk. 14:29). The charcoal fire burns on, and poor Peter stares into it, and remembers how, so recently, beside a similar fire, he had denied the Master three times. Three times the question is asked, but on the third occasion, the Lord changes the word for "love." Peter, in his responses, had not admitted to a strong settled disposition of love for Christ, but had avowed a love which was rather an emotion, "Lord . . . I am attached to Thee; I am fond of Thee." When the Lord changes to Peter's own word, Peter is grieved. "Is the Lord questioning even this in me?" he must have thought. "Lord, Thou knowest all things . . . "

Peter, the fisherman of the early part of the chapter, is now commissioned to be a shepherd. There is a hungry flock to be fed. There are little lambs to be tended. To the restored Peter the Lord commits the heavy, but sweet, responsibility: "Feed My lambs; shepherd My sheep; feed My sheep." I once asked a shepherd, "Why does our Lord mention the lambs first?" His answer, born of long experience with sheep and lambs, was this. "If the lambs are contented, then so is the flock; if the lambs are restless, the flock is restless too. Take care of the lambs, and you take care of the flock." May we follow His example who gently leads both sheep and lambs with shepherd love and care (Isa. 40:11).

The encouragement of the end part of John 21 is for those of us who may never be prominent either as fishermen or as shepherds. "Follow Me," says the risen Lord. We can all be disciples. "Till He come," may we faithfully wait and serve and follow.

The need to tend and feed the flock of God has never been greater.

Epilogue
He Ascended Up On High

Going to the Father

For thirty-three unique and wonderful years our Lord sojourned on earth. His was true Manhood; real humanity; but all stamped with moral perfection. From infancy, through boyhood, and youth, to holy maturity, He had lived fragrantly for His Father's pleasure. Every sacred footprint delighted the heart of God. Every step was hallowed. There had been, in this holy life, joy and sorrow mingled. There had been pain and pleasure, grief and glory. Now, on the road over Olivet, the last footprints were being impressed on the dusty path which He knew so well. "He led them out as far as to Bethany" (Lk. 24:50).

What precious memories this little town on the mount held for the Lord Jesus. When in so many other places He had been rejected, they had received Him at Bethany. Here they had shown Him hospitality, and He had enjoyed the warmth of their love. They had opened their homes and hearths and hearts to Him there. It had become for Him a haven in a world that had cast Him out. Is it coincidental, then, that as He prepared to leave earth, He led them out as far as to Bethany? Or does it not seem that He was reluctant to leave

Bethany, and when the moment of ascension arrived He would desire to leave His disciples in the atmosphere and spirit of the place that had so singularly received Him?

He lifted up His hands in priestly blessing upon them. We wonder what He said. His last words! His final benediction! He began to be parted from them. As they watched in sad silence, He rose from the midst of them with outspread, holy hands. Up and up; into the clouds; through the clouds; higher and higher; until at last, the Shekinah cloud itself took Him and hid Him from human view. He had gone up, and gone in, and sat down.

> *Hark those bursts of acclamation;*
> *Hark those loud, triumphant chords.*
> *Jesus takes the highest station;*
> *O what joy the sight affords.*
> *Crown Him! Crown Him!*
> *King of Kings and Lord of Lords.*

How little did the disciples realize at that moment the import of what had happened. A real Man had gone on high; into the heavens in His own right and by His own power. Of course, Enoch and Elijah had also gone up, but it was not the same. Our Lord ascended in personal power, with authority to do so. In defiance of natural law, and in defiance too of the prince of the powers of the air, "He ascended on high." He ascended, with every right to ascend, and heaven opened and received Him, and saluted Him, and adored Him. What are the implications of His ascension?

For the believer, it is full of encouragement and assurance. He has sat down. His work is done. Both He and His work are accepted. His sitting down is the pledge of that. And I am accepted in Him. God is satisfied, and rests, and I may rest too. And His presence in heaven is pledge of yet another thing. Because He is there, one day I shall be there too. "Where I am, there ye may be also" (Jn. 14:3). Here is the

Forerunner; He has gone in; we follow after.

For the Church, the ascension is a glorious truth. Christ, her Head, is in heaven, glorified. A new body has come into being; a great mystery; an *Ecclesia;* a heavenly people, a new creation. Consequent upon the ascension and glorification of the Son, the Spirit has been given, and with Him, those gifts to men from the risen Head. Did not our Lord say, "It is expedient for you that I go away" (Jn. 16:7)?

For the devil, the implications of the ascension are solemn. The enthronement of Christ is the judgment of the prince of this world. The ascended One is far above all principalities, and powers, and might, and dominion, and every name that is named. Satan is annulled. The glorification of the Son spells the doom of the wicked one. God, in exalting Jesus, has judged the usurper. With the judgment of the prince of this world, the world too, stands indicted. It stands charged with the sin of unbelief which rejected the Saviour. That righteousness of Christ, which men failed to see and acknowledge, is now proven. The Father has received the righteous One in glory, and He is vindicated (Jn. 16:8-11).

> *Man of Sorrows, God of Glory,*
> *Wondrous path Thy foot hath trod;*
> *Cross and crown rehearse the story,*
> *Joyful sound this note abroad:*
> *Calvary's Victim*
> *Now adorns the Throne of God.*

We recall again the words of the beloved C. H. M., "The study of the Lord Himself, in His ways among men, bows the heart in worship, and fills the soul with wonder." We trust it has been so, as we have sought to trace the footprints of the Saviour.